George Me

I'M HAVING THE RHYME OF MY LIFE

GEORGE MELLING
Poems and Tales by Th'Owd Chap

"TH'OWD CHAP"

KEEP SMILING

X

Talentvine Press

Published in 2017 by Talentvine Press

ISBN 978-1-9999438-0-6

Design by Flapjack Press
flapjackpress.co.uk

Printed by Imprint Digital
Upton Pyne, Exeter, Devon
imprintdigital.com

Remembering
Stephen and Alwyn.

They are why I write poetry.

We are of our laughs and sorrows,
what happened yesterday
is with us today
and governs our tomorrows.

2002 and 2007
R.I.P.

*Dedicated
to
Ar Sharon,*

*fellow performer,
literary editor,
unofficially adopted daughter,
carer,
photographer
and dearest friend.*

Contents

I'M HAVING THE RHYME OF MY LIFE

A talk written for the Everyman Theatre, in Liverpool,
as part of a programme called Platform, performed on 12th May 2016.

I'm just George, oil refinery worker, a lovely wife, Alwyn,
son Stephen, who developed grand-mal epilepsy as a child,
mild learning difficulties, dyslexia, sports mad,
played badminton for his college,
won trophies for snooker and pool.

Dad and son watch Wigan Athletic and Wigan Rugby together,

Alwyn likes an occasional game of bingo,

own house in Wigan, nice garden, two lovely cats,

mi life revolves round mi family,
if they're happy, I'm happy.

Then suddenly ... Alwyn collapses,
turns out to be inoperable spinal cord damage,
long spell in hospital, then home.
Now, a wheelchair user for life.

Do you know,
mi Alwyn had been helping disabled young folks for years,
just doesn't seem fair, took us time to adjust, but ... we did,
still a family, still enjoyed ourselves,
still wrapped up in one another ...

I woke up at 4am this morning,
rushed for mi pad and pen.
Poetry controls the poet,
NOT the other way round ...

Lost Dreams Revisited

I only see a black sunrise,
this childhood excursion of
bucket and spade,
and
donkey
and
bathe.

I only see a black sunset,
this once was
"kiss me quick" hat,
rock
and
promenade

and memory of
seaside,
and
laughter
and
unwind
turns to an icy grip
of
despair and sorrow,
and
each tomorrow

that leads to today
reminds me,
holidays can be fun
with
family together,

and
sea
and sun,

but
sunrise
and
sunset,
each gazed at vista of wonder
and stare,
has now
turned to black
in this emotion
laid bare
of a memory share,
with lost family.

Stephen, our only son,
passed away whilst on holiday with us in Blackpool.

Holidays used to be lovely,
now
I only see a black sunrise.

We'd gone to Blackpool for two weeks.
On the Monday of the second week,
August 5th, 2002,
a date stamped into mi brain,
sheer unimaginable, indescribable despair.

In the poem called 'Holiday', which I perform on mi CD of poetry
(brought out with the help of Producer/Musician Stephen Houghton
and Musician James Mahmoud on behalf of Wigan and Leigh
Hospice), I explain about Stephen's passing.

Me and mi Alwyn,
God knows how we carried on,
but we did,

because we had one another,
and I had to carry on because I was
Alwyn's carer as well as her husband,
so
we got into our own little routine,

but
holidays were out,
not after Stephen's passing.

Instead
we went to concerts,
Take That,
Johnny Mathis,
Neil Diamond,
Tom Jones,
Elton John,
Rod Stewart,
etc, etc ...

I've never been back to Wigan Athletic on mi own,
some things I can't face.

Of course
we were broken,
heartbroken,
but we ploddered on,
until ... 5 years later
mi lovely Alwyn,
mi reason for carrying on,
passed away suddenly ...

Another Day to Pause

to unscramble thought
and limb,

another dawn to gaze
blue-skied glow,
this heaven sent hymn

without word,

just a quiet time of day
to sit,
to reflect,
to wonder
what's it all about?

This window viewed beauty
with its gentle hug
and
quiet shout

that screams
"good morning"
to an old chap,

still working on his jigsaw,
not many pieces to go
but faster
and faster

and fas ... ... t ... ... e ... ... r ... ...

It was hard, still is sometimes, but
through mi music and poetry,
and good friends ...

14 years ago
mi only son died.

9 years ago
mi wife died ...

and this 'Owd Chap died ... almost,
he retreated, his innermost,
like a flower closes in on itself,
but slowly,

as each dark day turned into week,
as each passing month a life spark seek,
slowly,
through mi memory and tear,
I unfolded, each new year.

Through writing and word,
and being heard,

I'm able to stand here,

and share mi die, and share mi stories,
and share mi cry, and share mi glories,

and all through our love of poetry.

Tonight,
I've collected a new memory, this Owd Chap,
this born-again pensioner.

14 years ago mi only son died,

9 years ago mi wife died,

14 years later I'm here,
to quietly and humbly say,

thank you for giving me a voice,
for listening,
for helping me to live again,
and for sharing
mi memories.

Manchester Arena and a Suicide Bomber

It seems my journey from the horrors of the
Second World War
still trembles on that
rocky road of hate ...
as we remember those 22 people killed
and
those 64 people injured.

When mi son Stephen died,
me and Alwyn,
because we couldn't face going on holiday,
attended many concerts at the Arena,
we knew a lot of the staff who always went out of their way to
help an Old Chap and wheelchair dependent wife ...
and now,
a 73 years old widower,
sad beyond words.

Tentative shuffle out mi front door,
№17,
and a first gulp of
not poison gas
but
the happy thoughts of a yellow tulip
yawning and stretching an
"I'm here"
a today greeting of simple,
of creation,
of beauty,
of peace,
of rebirth
and I veer to an angry blackbird
chirping and waiting

to be fed,
as if an entitlement.

A tentative shuffle out mi front door
to my little world
without
suicide bomb,
without
genocide,
without
power struggle and
killing and rape
and
fleeing to a better life that when reached
doesn't always welcome them.

Just an old chap from the horrors of
the Second World War
still trying to make sense of this world.

I remember the giant steps of the first man on the moon,
the birth of the NHS,
my first open-mouthed look at this new thingy called television,
me and mi son playing rugby
and going to watch Wigan Athletic together,
and
Aberfan and Hillsborough and Lockerbie and
the day mi son died ...
and
5 years later, mi wife,

and that Monday night ,
an indelible memory of futile ideology
and twisted evil,
of grief and pain and horror
and fractured lives,

and a blanket of love as we come together
to condemn, to comfort,
to offer a hand of friendship and peace.

I need to stand in mi garden
to be reminded ...
we are blessed with a beautiful world,

it's just sometimes,
it doesn't seem so.

Letter to my Son 1

Happy 51st Birthday, Stephen,
and as the years creep along to once again
a soon to start new season ...
your beloved Wigan Warriors on their path to glory,
I hope today will be one of ...

that wished for present,
a game of snooker,
customary cake,

all topped off with a day
free from your epilepsy,
that you never let
intrude on
enjoying life,

and the icing on your uncomplicated little world ...
a Big Mac.

Letter to my Son 2

Happy birthday Stephen,
on what would have been your
51st birthday
if illness hadn't intervened
15 years ago.

I miss you.

Dad, alone with his memories, 23rd January 2017.

Dear Agony Aunt ...
A true story.

I had a bone-shaker bike
with Sturmey-Archer 3-speed gears,
nine year old lad,
leather threadbare saddle with
bare springs.

We wuz poor,
shorts with holes ...
no underpants.

Cycling uphill, Lamberhead Road,
panting,
stopped to get mi breath,
then it happened ...

a spring clamped onto mi left bollock.

As a mature gent
I still have nightmares,

what do you recommend?

*Dear Sir,
your letter pains me
as it obviously did you.
Get a donkey
and stop talking testicles.*

My days are split up with ... sticky toffee pudding, naked gardening ...
it's true, ask mi photographer, Ar Sharon. Are you still in therapy?
And unsolicited phone calls, you don't know who'll you'll meet.

Just Had a Phone Call

"Excuse me please,
how are you?"
Foreign accent,
possibly St. Helens on a wet day.

"We've received the information
that someone at this address
has been involved in an accident
in the last few weeks.
Is that right please?"

I said,
"Yes,

I was driving down mi street last week
and mi neighbour,
he was having a quick meat and potato pie,
he'd walked to his own car clutching it in his left hand
because he'd left his teeth in't glove box
but he had to reach over from the driver's side
because his passenger door is dodgy,
he popped the pie,
still in its little case,
on't road just as I was gathering speed
and I felt the slight squelch as
I squashed the poor thing ...

Are you ringing about that?"

"Or,
last month,
on Ainsdale Beach,
contemplating
is it fair to other people
to don mi Speedos
and
power walk to the retreating sea,
when I swerved to avoid a crab
and ended up
in Crosby
and collided with an iron man ...

Are you ringing about that?"

"Or,
I was taken short on Rivington Moor,
and just as the full sun
shone on Uranus
an over sixties hiking club,
clutching their bus passes and
on their first geocache exercise,
thought I was the next landmark
and posted their trinkets and tokens in
what they thought was a natural fissure in
the cliff face ...

Are you ringing about that?"

"Or,
I was on top of a ladder
Artexing mi back kitchen ceiling,
the phone kept ringing,
I climbed all the way down
to answer the sodding thing ..."

"Excuse me please,
how are you?"
Foreign accent, possibly St. Helens, still raining.
I flung the receiver down in anger
and it badly lacerated mi left foot
and whilst on mi way to
Accident and Emergency
I had severe thoughts about
sticking the phone
up your arse if we
ever meet up ...

"Are you ringing about that?"

At which point he said something in Urdu
and it wasn't ... "have a good day",

and seriously hung up.

I wonder why?

Just Seen a Plumpy Robin

Just seen a plumpy robin
at mi feeding station,

it twittered contentedly,

it didn't utter racist bile,

it didn't repeat gutter press garbage about Jeremy,

it didn't say, "thank you", for my help ...
but there again ...
it didn't shit on me.

Just seen a plumpy robin
at mi feeding station,

it twittered contentedly.

I'd been to St. Helens, performing mi poetry, first time there for me,
and a few hours later, in bed and in a blaze of blood, lumpy retreated
back into mi inner sanctum.
Now, I'm not saying it was the shock of being in St. Helens on a dark,
cold Sunday night, but there again ...

If You've Got a Lump, Go To St. Helens

It was as if mi brain,
sod this for a lark, mate,
71 years,
no chance of parole,

I want to see,
not just imagine,
oh ... hello,
here I am,
like a mole,

a sodding lump
just above mi right eye,

so you do, don't you?
Think all sorts, fear,

is this it?
Oh dear.

So it sat,
or clung,
or abseiled
and grew,
like mi anxiety ... grew,

no pain,
no noise,

no wriggle,
no ... good morning,
just benign
like a sign
of menace,

expanding ... the unknown,
the ... what's round the next corner,
in this case
what's on mi bleeding head,
thoughts of ... impending dead,

I know mi rights,
been locked away
like an after-thought,

your mechanics,
your impulse,
your yearning,

your compassion,
your create,
your learning,

your dark side,
your charity,
your sweetness ... and light,

your loving,
your sadness,
your shyness ... and fight,

your memory.

Talking about memory, brainy,
can we have a word?

Talking about memory, brainy,
can we have a word?

Talking about ... ...

So there it sat,
one day,
two days,
and ... it
grew,

three days,
four days,
like it ...
knew,
can't unscrew,

a week,
two weeks,
each daily view,
third week,
I eschew
looking
at this alien,
mocking,
living
part of me that
each mirror's reflect
I still see,

until,

mi poetry,
St. Helens,
and
perform,

then home,
and bed
and ...
brainstorm,

at least
lumpy ... storm,
was hanging by a thread
in a haze of red
blood,

then it's gone ... for good,

I hope?

An Easter Sunday story.
Love and peace and friendship and family
are the threads that bind.

Easter Sunday, St. Joseph's and a Faint Echo of Memory

I can escape yesterday's
pain and move forwards
but I don't forget ...

Memories of Easter long ago,
Stephen and his boxed chocolate egg
with two pound coins taped to the outside edge,
new pair of trainers
and promise of a ride
to the far flung reaches of his world,
Arthur Silcock's amusement arcade,
Central Prom, Blackpool,
where,
clutching his bag of ten pences,
escapes into his world of
lemons and plums and cherries
randomly spinning to the rhythm of his concentration ...

Alwyn, breakfast in bed,
cuddly Easter Bunny
and the safe embrace of her family
lulls into what can go wrong ...?

And if they're happy, I'm happy,
I'll always be here for them,
a protective embrace of safety and care
except that I wasn't, twice,
and I'll share this Easter Sunday with just mi thoughts,

and maybe I can hear
the faint echoes
of worship from a forgotten other family ...

as the rows upon rows of
terraced 2 up, 2 downs,
the Ropemakers Arms
and Westhead's toffee shop,
a close knit community crowding Wallgate

all razed and broken up
to be replaced by retail units,

a spreading out of its flock
signalled the
death knell
of St. Joseph's R.C. Church,
a grade 2 listed building
in the shadow of
Wigan Pier.
Empty shelled centre of prayer
forlorn, deserted years ago,
towers rotting and lonely and bare,
an Easter congregation no more.

Stands Joseph ... his sentinel perch
on high, absent flock to greet,
stone eyes, a Christian search
but despairs of a welcome meet.

A church in look but not deed,
deconsecrated, decrepit, dead,
once welcomed neighbours in need
to provide a message that fed

an innate need for worship

to praise their God on high,
a coming together in fellowship
until that final goodbye.

Bare brick, missing tiles, roof leak,
smashed windows that once inspired,
now barely elicits a peek
Kingdom of God
long ago
retired.

George Formby Junior, our famous son of Wigan,
attended Sunday School there.

St. Joseph's served its last Mass on 22nd October, 1995.
Another anniversary to rekindle memory and remind us to cherish
what we've got in case it's no longer there.

Pemberton Central Ward Labour Club

roofless   soulless   member-less

This working man's refuge
from a day of toil,
hen-pecked husband's retreat
and safety foil
from her who rules his roost,

and Cissie and Ada,
same two chairs booked,
bingo nights each week
when eyes down they looked,
it provided a boost

the bland and struggle
and weekly muddle
of just living,

the price of a drink,
escape kitchen sink
and barely a misgiving

of time spent
concert night,
where couples, their weekly
highlight
from the mundane

to a world
of committee,
a peace
and a sanctity
and the chairman's reign

with a rod of iron,
occasionally the scion
of change

until change came,
fixture of its community, self-same,
is in disarrange.

Roof's gone, just an empty shell
signals the death knell
of an artery,

bare lights dangle
from an empty beamed tangle
of memory,

each hammer blow
signals a slow
drifting apart of community,

each felled wall
an angry call
of disunity,

this working class temple of lore,
people's beacon of hope,
no more.

Pemberton Central Ward Labour Club
in Enfield Street
is being demolished
to make way for town houses,

but strangely,
from inside this empty, roofless shell,
multi-coloured disco lights
continue to flash,

maybe a cry of pain,
or a last goodbye
from a loyal servant ...

until they too,
its last beating heart,
finally fade.

Our Mum

Two of mi mates,
their mum,
she's passed on,
and his children know
with full age,
this icon,

strength and support
their lifeblood,
who dressed their wound,

soothed those tears,
clothed and fed,
illness kept immune,

or cold compress
their fevered brows
gently bathed,

and they know
their mum,
who swathed

her love
around them
without limit,

her credo,
her daily mantra,
her remit,

a mum,
a support,
always there,

except now

for just this once
she's passed elsewhere,

and her children know,
but it's still
hard,

it's upsetting,
it's sad,
like a discard,

to sever
those bonds
and let go,

but, we all know
it's the ultimate
love,
our owe,

this last act
of arrangement
and tribute,

our honouring
of our mum,
our contribute

to say thank you,
and now it's your time,
that time we all fear,

we'll be okay
your children,
in spite of
our tear.

Sometimes, we think they're invincible,
until ... suddenly ... they're not here.

Mi mate Petya had never been outside England
since arriving from Bulgaria some years back ...
So, on her birthday ...

A Scottish Adventure

Here we are ... Coach D ... seats 25 and 26 ...
Wigan to Edinburgh, Trans-Pennine Express, 6.43am,
a windowed gateway to
rolling hills,
distant mist strewn mountains,
hot air balloon over Penrith,
lonely farmhouse
and ...

contented cows
munching the hours
'til their next milk.

Eddie Stobart truck
waving goodbye to our
ever speeding faces
as it drives
a lonely road,

and an
interminably
stupid and hypnotic
musical torment emanating
from a juvenile's electronic game ...

and where
the soft Scottish lilt of our nice lady guard,
politely asking us to respect
our fellow passengers enjoyment

of a stress free journey,
and keep noise levels down ...
hasn't reached him,
maybe due to
a childhood starvation
of
Iron Bru,

breaking our spell of
tranquillity
as we approach ...

Locarbaidh (Lockerbie),
that place of
Pan Am flight 103
carrying
Abdelbaset al-Mehrahi,
forever gouged
in our memory,
as it was on the town.

With a clickety click
and a clickety clack,
as Wigan we left,
this Scottish bound track,

and the miles gobbled up
each town we passed,
each station appeared
the same as each last,

this movement of luggage
and people, constant change,
as homeward some go
and outward some range,

and a clickety click
and a clickety clack,
in mi head at least
as mi memory miles back,

to steam train and shovel
and boiler and coal,
now smoothness and quiet
as nearer our goal

with each moving vista
of valley and hill,
of wind farm and sheep
and travel time kill,

trapped as we are
our busy lives each,
as passengers in a train
'til destination ...
reach.

A journey of opposites,
sleepy hamlets,
industry,
wind farms,
rivers and contented cattle
all bathed in sun
and
country air,
and

Carstairs,
a prison of the mind
waves a sorrowful hello and goodbye,
whose residents are locked
from society

by the extra addition
of
a security fence ...
keeping us out,

as onwards we speed
with a cream and brown and grey approach
to Margadh An Fheòir (Haymarket),
until
a dignified City arrival
signifies
journeys end
and
adventure begin
on the

Wigan to Edinburgh
Trans Pennine Express
at
9.37 am,
on a sunny Monday
in August,

with a supporting cast of:

The National Gallery of Scotland,
street artists and musicians,
Henderson's vegan restaurant,
Edinburgh Castle ...

but,
not the chap in their ticket office
who thought it alright
to upload a handful of
5p coins
in this 'Owd Chap's change ...

so ...
up yours,
I hope your Trossachs
get wrapped round
your sporran.

Princess St. Gardens,
and
an A-Z map of the city,
at least 50 years old ...
why replace if not broken?

The map that is ... and me.

A Jam Butty

on a
doorstop wedge,
together with
"eat your veg",
it's what got us through the privations
of our war
and post-war
years
and the tears
of
hunger,

that grey period of
six inch nail behind lavvy door
adorned with little squares of the
Daily Mirror
and well before,
and I'd never heard of it 'til
I reached eleven,
bog roll,

those chickenless
and lamb joint less
days of
Spam and
Tripe and
Brawn,
born
out of the togetherness of
make the best,

of empty street
devoid of three cars to a family

where magic feet
dribbled and passed and scored
and imagined crowd roared
in what became
Anfield or
Old Trafford or
for Kieron, mi mate,
Bootle F.C.
where we footied
until she,
that dreaded cry of mams ...

"George, get in, now!"

And the star centre forward, me,
would have to be substituted by he,
strolling by,
a useless lolloper from t'other avenue,
bottle of dandelion and burdock
and
coltsfoot rock
and on an errand to get a
penny mantle for't
gas light,
looks like his family will have to sit a bit longer
in their dark,
stark
back kitchen
such is the importance of these big
floodlit games,
courtesy of the
slow
hiss and warm glow
of a street lamp,
and "see in the dark" eyes
thanks to mam's advice

of
"eat your carrots".

A jam butty,
the star of our school dinner,
where the better off would scoff and stare
and mock
and glare
the cruelty of
have and have not.

A jam butty
that filled our rickety bones,
postponed
an expectant belly
and cured all manner of illness
in that austere time of
pre National Health,
a wealth
that nowadays
we take for granted ...

A jam butty that
mi breakfast
I've just had
with a tad
of nostalgia
as I roll back these 73 years,
stark remembrance of war fears
and the tears
for absent menfolk
spoke
about with barely a whisper,

content with your lot
cause nobody else got,

or so we thought
but
the reality was different
as we now know
in this present of
show
life
as it is,
warts and all.

A jam butty that reminds ....
happiness is only a slice away
on this new day
of
the rest of mi life.

Not just a jar of homemade jam, but a memory of rickety ladder,
sun dappled orchard and steaming pans
lorded over by two good mates - Ian and Annette,
Lord and Lady of a beautiful barn conversion
somewhere in the wilds of Hindley/Aspull.

First Wigan Diggers' committee meeting last night,
the luxurious surroundings of The Anvil,
after a successful Festival 2017, chaired by Joe who took no prisoners,
any other business ...

George, damson jam, this is for you,
and I clutched it for the rest of the evening as if a bottle of best
Bourbon,
to be sampled this morning on a wedge,
Asda's best Mediterranean bread, cup of Costa Rican
and memories back to a 1940s council estate
when getting old
wasn't an option.

Another Place
Anthony Gormley's Iron Men, Crosby Beach.

Iron strong, their stares of dream,
beyond the waves to distant shore,
face wakening dawn , this team,
bathed twice a day, in ebb and flow.

Watery home atop mother beach,
and sentinels ... ships come and go,
a silent message of hope, to reach,
these iron men, and their silent tableau.

Is it a welcome, their eager eyes
and hand of friendship, reach out,
or, do they wave, their last goodbyes
to fading memories, their lookout?

Another time, another place, another dream of home,
this army marches, in one spot, a witness, hope for all,
home is where our heart is, wherever we may roam,
across this mighty sea-way,
until
our
own
landfall.

A Feline Trilogy

I
Do You Remember ...? Miaoww

Do you remember, miaoww,
a shy little kitty
hiding under reams of fabrics,
behind
and inclined
on top,
with barely a peep
and leap
and scuttle
and disappear for a while
until
a mobile
pair of eyes
size
up,

who's this visitor to mi mum's studio?

A tentative creep
to reap
carefully positioned biscuits
because Grandad knew food
could be the way
to say

"Hello".

Do you remember
a shy little kitty visited,
mum in tow,

№17's unfamiliar door
to disappear in a dark corner
escape the stress of change
as we range
from that what I know,
to an unaccustomed hello
and
now and again
those same little pairs of questioning eyes
that spies,
a tentative glimpse ,
a proffered biscuit to convince
a pretty young lady,
let's be friends.

Then,
do you remember, miaoww,
that fateful day,
I came to stay
for a few days,
mi mum,
something called income,
driving full time poet Dominic
around the fleshpots of
Cumbria,
and me and mi cardboard suitcase
face
the portal of №17
and 5 days of hide,
not eat,
hide,
not eat again,
hide,
and a Grandad going scatty with worry
as I, from mi lair,
cock a snook

and make him look
here, there,
everywhere ...

but slowly,
a bond,
a routine,
a relaxing of care
as I dare
to say,
miaoww, hello Grandad,
any chance of a play ...?

'til mum's return
and back home.

II
A Kitten ... A Suitcase ... A Team

Laser light is Buttons new toy,
four legged, furry Usain Bolt,
flying fur ... occur ... across room,
her quest, sodding pin-prick , assault.

Roll over ... her belly display,
miniature toy straddling four legs,
laughing eyes, a squeak, a cuddle,
a chat, as each day begs

our Grandad and Buttons ... a team,
sharing of mischief, glad heart,
but each day signals that time
when she and her suitcase depart,

and my house, once more, quiet
will descend ... an eerie calm,

but these last few days, at least,
imprinted memory,
special
kitty ma'am.

But
I liked it really,
a little girl
to twirl
Grandad
round mi little paw,
to play on command
and demand
a brush,
biscuits whenever
and as for
sodding fussy with mi food ...
whatever.

Do you remember, miaoww,
that time,

as mi mum, Calais,
film unit to record
the discord,
the flight
and plight
of refugees,

as I
two weeks of
feeding time strop,
and top
of the oven
mi choice of bed
as I led
a merry dance,

a chance
once again to just be me,
find the kitty as I hid
and bid
poor Grandad to exclaim,
where the hell are you,

but slowly a bond,
a love beyond
a visit,
and

do you remember, miaoww,
that fateful day,
litter tray
in tow,
I arrived ... mi new home,
to blend
and spend
mi future,
not losing a mum
but
gaining a Grandad
to greet
and meet
a feeding bowl of welcome ...
Where's mi tea?
As he
smiles a contented smile.

III
What is a Cat?

A cat is four legs
and a tail
of

speed
and chase,

a cat is two eyes
and a nose
of
sniff
and grace

with her presence.

Here I am,
I've eaten,
plucked carpet,
I've licked,
now
you'll submit,

me time,
for a brush
and a rush ... and jump

nearest shelf,
nearest chairback,
nearest window,
with that knack

of delicate,
of sleek,
of unhurried,
of a look of ... meek.

Look at me,
aren't I clever?
Ohhh,

was you having a read?
Whatever!!

A cat is
the centre of your life,

to love,
and care,
and talk,

and share
your
worries.

A cat is ...
whoever you want it to be.

Grandad's and mum's cat is ...

Buttons.

McDonald's, Mi Mate Michael and Leonie

An elderly gentleman at large with the Wigan Diggers
the night before the Festival,
a darkening Wiend as the gazebos arise from the ashes
and Janet is heard to shout,
as if in an exclusive men's club in London ...

"Can everyone grab a leg and,
right a bit,
left a bit,
come to me,
back off,
drop."

I stand,
more a hindrance than help,
book and pen and imbuing an
air of calm
amidst the chaos and temper
and sampling of a fully working bar
and blackening sky
and a lone voice squeaks ...

"I'm starving,
could murder a fillet o' fish large meal
with fries and
strawberry milkshake."

"I'll have a walk down,
Ar Sharon."
Nice young lady,
"Can I help you please?"
"I'd like a fillet o'
large fr ...
straw ... ... milks ...

and can you pop them in a carrying bag
because I'm with the Diggers gang up the hill
getting ready for tomorrow's Festival
and mi hand's not very good
these days."

"Mi granddad told me about that,
I'm working tomorrow until 5pm
but me and mi boyfriend will try and go,
thanks for reminding me,
here's your order,
can you manage to carry them in
this little bag with handles?"

"Thank you young lady,
you've been very kind,
I'll look for you both tomorrow."

Back up the hill to a starving Sharon
and the busy chaos that's slowly
coming together into tent city.

Next day,
full swing with crowd and
music and performance and
trade display ...

"Hello Michael,"
as mi mate waves and approaches me,
garbed as I am for the day,
period costume, staff in hand,
ever open doored to
selfies and chats.

"Hiya George,
mi granddaughter Leonie
works at McDonald's

was telling me a nice old gentleman,
a customer, last night,
was telling her all about today."

I said,
"Sounds like someone I know,"
just a simple story, those threads in life
that wrap around our shoulders
and comfort,
and a kind young lady
shining a beacon of hope
from the generation that follows
me.

Mi Big Shop (or Trouble and Squeak)
The highlight of mi week.

Squeak ... squeak,

trolleys to the left of me,
trolleys to the right of me,
sodding trolleys in mi face,
this showplace,

squeak ... squeak,

of
grimace
and
pace
to be first to't sodding baked beans
and vegan fish fingers
and woe betide he who lingers,

squeak ... squeak,

this mad,
couldn't care less
get out of mi way ...
shove,
lunge,
place
of shopping frenzy.

*"Colleagues to the check-out,
any spare bods to the tills please"*

before
a riot occur

and
customers dare
to give up ...

sans patience,
sans cheese ...
and
sans cat food,

and
Quorn sausages,
bread rolls,
Asda own brand
bog rolls ...

Rissoles ...
to the lot
of them.

I hate shopping,
this place of
rush
and pile
and grab
and dare to smile ...

squeak ... squeak,

"Security,
a happy customer
aisle 4,
suggest
exit door ..."

'Cause they don't,
do they?

An air of happiness imbue,
war of wills test
an elderly gent
hell bent
on chaos,
because he's good at

sucking his soup through a straw,
weeding,
fighting off mortis rigor
and needing

help
now on his own
with
the peril of age,
a rampage
through life's story
and turning a page
not of glory
but,
mi shopping list,

and,
mi trolley's got a right-hand bias,
a Tory trolley,
riding rough-shod
and scattering bodies
in its aftermath ...

and a

squeak ... squeak,

as I seek ...

It wuz here last week,
and the week before,
and every week,
'til
suddenly,
hide and seek,

they've moved everything
miserable sods,
as I grunt and shunt
this unwelcomed treasure hunt,
and clutch at thin air
that what was there
but
not anymore ...

I confront ...

"Excuse me,
Tunnock's Tea Cakes,
they was here last week,
now a peek
says,
where the hell are they?"

As the Asda colleague,
for the thousandth time today ...

a customer irate,
and late
for
his empty day spread out,
as if important,
but still,
the antics of this supermarket will ...
piss him off.

"They're in aisle 44
with the baby nappies
and anti-diarrhoea tablets,
panty liners
vegan spread,
soda bread,
Sudafed
and
sewing thread."

What about Fiery Jack ...?
and we seem to have a lack
of Sudocrem,
and
don't get those two
mixed up,
tears to mi eyes
signifies
flaming heck ...
that's
a
hot
bot.

Of course they are,
why didn't I think of that
as I doff mi cap
and let one go ... *(fart)*
and hope the aisle ... *(fart)*
(I'd had a curry)
stays empty ... *(fart)*
(a big curry)
until I turn the corner,

"Cleaner to aisle 13 ... Spillage."

squeak ... squeak,

and that little old lady
shuffling along in her
Cosyfeet slippers
and carrying
two carrots,
one potato,
an onion
and
a bottle of Newcastle Brown
in her basket
will be blamed for the smell.

It's mi age ...

squeak ... squeak,

Whatever happened to the corner shop?
It's ...

*"Good morning, sir.
What can I get you?"*

An ambient air
of unrush
without crush,
familiar stock
and
Coltsfoot Rock,
and
no

"Unexpected item in the bagging area."

squeak ... squeak,

And I reminisce,
and spot
a pretty young thing,
probably getting her partner's tea,
frozen dinner for one
and
let's see,

bottle of Strongbow,
kill his urges
cause she knows
it's been a fortnight without,
and
he gets fruity
and
her duty ...
So,
she'd best get custard creams
and kill
his dreams,
at least for tonight ...

And at the approach of mi

squeak ... squeak,

shoppers flee
and mi trolley
weaves ...
an irregular inspection,
sudden correction,
or stop,
as mi list is carefully perused
until ...

"Unexpected item in the bagging area."

And I answer back,
"are you talking to me?
Do you feel lucky ... punk?"

as the young lady assistant says ...
with a voice
as if she's talking to
a high-backed chair,
resident of,
with drool running down mi chin,

"Do you need help with your packing, luv?"

Well,
Have mi underpants got skid marks?
Do I look in the first flush of youth?
Am I a cantankerous 'owd pensioner?

"Ohh,
yes please,
that's very kind of you."

And I

squeak ... squeak,

across the car park,
half a mile to mi Micra,

until I remember,
it wasn't
Tunnock's Tea Cakes,
they were last week, but
Cadbury's Flakes ...

Ohh bollocks!!!!

*"Unexpected item ... Again ...
in the sodding bagging area."*

Squeak ... squeeeeeeeeak!

*I sat outside with a bottle of whisky one early December night, late
into the evening, still struggling after the death of mi son, and then mi
wife. Strangely, mi new shed put mi life into perspective,
for that evening at least, or it could have been the 40% spirit talking.*

Mi Down Poem ... I Wrote It As I Felt It

Mi new shed's just a shed,
but it's something else,
it's mi future,

it's me saying, I'm not finished,
mi old shed's been demolished,
this on mi own, I've accomplished,
part of mi old life's vanished,

and this is what we do,
push forward, carry on, stiff upper lip,
but sometimes, like now, 11 o'clock at night,
taking sanctuary in a bottle,
just noticed mi shed and thought, well done,
new life's begun,
is there, out there, anyone

just to notice me?
Say to themselves, he needs help,
can't demolish him and replace for new,
as slowly, drip by drip, withdrew.
Tries his best, music, poetry,
move forward, keep active, self-worth,
back end of life rebirth,
trying hard not to be stillbirth.

Is it mi bottle talking,
or is it me,

am I getting alcohol maudlin
or have I a right to plea
this, our world we live, evacuee,
can I excuse myself, absentee
in mi own world, flee?

Because it's not easy,
can't let go,
too many memories,
too many struggles, and loves, and sharing,
can't suddenly, memory erase, not caring,
heartache open and baring,
past life not a shed,
can't take down and replace,
but an emotion, a love, a reason,
as natural as year and season.

And whilst mostly, friends say,
he's doing okay,
deep hidden is mayday,
and his future ... just today.

Sat here, me and mi bottle friend,
it would be nice, message of hope send,
but I feel down, sinking, lost,
but not unvoiced,
at least my words ... you hear,
not alone, other people, feel near,
perhaps tomorrow, new day, new hope,
clear head, put away bottle, and cope.

This is my dark poem,
when the night was dark,
when I was dark,
is my spirit dark?
Will the morning bring light?

Will it bring new fight?
Will my soul relight?

Is my bottle half full?

Or half empty?

Or just ... ... empty?

A quick press of the handle
and all our guilty pleasures ...
float away on a tide of nostalgia.
On a diet again ... are we?

Ode to a Number Two

I "went",

and there it lay ...
or floated,
small to medium,
no ...
definitely small,

it'd done its best
in the reduced circumstances,

lonely ... but dignified,
glancing up from its watery shield,
and soon to be flushed ... with relief,

but not before the question
bowled at me
as if in toilet humour ...

on a diet again... are we?

The Road from Wigan Pier

Cast of characters:
Dave the Security from Chester
Tim Foster the Nikon
Th'Owd Chap, professional poser
Ar Sharon
Malik the waiter
a defecating dog
various bemused motorists

Been anywhere nice?

Disabled brother's,
Dave the Council,
shower room conversion,

then Boots at Robin Park retail park,
gents' incontinence pants,
£7.99 pack of twelve,
£3 off voucher, beauty products,

Poundworld,
colour changing solar garden lights

then
back to mi car
stifling a yawn
and a fart
and a twinge
of a simple day ...

tap, tap, tap,

"Shit,
I'm being mugged!"

"Hello,
hope you don't mind
but
can I do a photoshoot?"
A tall, bristled, lumbering, unexpected Mr. Nikon ...

I'm out like a shot,
say
"Would you like a poem?"
and
his camera hyperventilates
a succession of
clicks and flashes
as I pirouette
and
pout
and
recite
and balance
this way,
that way,
any way I can spot an audience in the retreating cars
and slightly bemused drivers,
a touch more accelerator than healthy ...

whilst foaming at the mouth,
Tim the Nikon ...

By this stage he knows mi name,
mi writings,
our mutual friends,
what I'd had for mi breakfast
and

mi waist size,

and
the fact I'd performed mi new poem
for the first time last night in New Brighton,
I'll give you a sniff of it ...

* * *

One Sheet or Three?

or four
or
more
this daily chore,
excepting when
bunged up the flow
of discarded pleasure,

today's imponderable
as
a never ending supply of tissue
carefully balanced
and
swiped and wiped

peered,
and jeered
back
as if to say ...

not done yet?

The bog roll
gets
thinner

as
yesterday's dinner,
now
an unwanted inconvenience,
stares up
languidly,

on another day
paper outlay
diminished
as
one sheet
or two
will do
the job,

but today,
wipe
and peer,
wipe and
leer
back
as if to say
haha,
try again ...

then
wipe
and peer
and leer
again
and
again
and leer
and peer ...
until

sod it
and
sodding shit
and a rush to
flush
the evidence ...

and flush
the evidence ...

and fl ... u ... s ... h
t ... h ... e
evi ... den ... ce ...

* * *

I'm performing,
he's flashing,

whilst approaching ...
high viz man,

"Excuse me,
the shops have sent me over,
they're observing
and
getting a touch twitchy,
is everything alright
only
we can see an old man tottering
and
muttering
and possibly getting a touch of the
assaults ..."

"No, no, no,"

I explained,
then
to high viz Dave, security ...
I told the tale of my visit to Chester ...

* * *

I descended from the roman wall,
strolled down to the river
and became part of its fabric ...
for the length of this poem.

The Song of the River

Cormorants, wings raised aloft,
like a washing day, clothes abreast,
straddling weir on River Dee,
sentinel straight, in a line, at rest.

The roar of the water cascade,
occasional ripple, airborne bird,
slows down a speeding life,
as the natural rhythms heard.

I stand and look and refresh,
commune with this scene unfold,
just me, a river, some birds,

and a story

waiting

to be told.

* * *

Then a poem written on Halloween.
Clinging to the ancient walls of Chester
can be heard the whispered columns of hundreds
marching the years, until today ...

Halloween Meets the Ghosts of a City Wall

Roman wall that straddles the height,
this historic city I'm found,
on a day that nurtures fright,
full circle, the ramparts bound.

Half way, Red Lion, a snack,
lost calories I'm keen renew,
'til satiated, to the wall back,
as each gate portfolios new view.

Amphitheatre, multi-toilet to share,
and I stroll wide-eyed each sight,
sheer drop, have a peek, dare,
looms building, costumed black and white,

with the inscription:

"The fear of the Lord is a fountain of life."

On Halloween, with ghosts of past,
an army of spirits I greet,
Roman garrison, trick or treat cast,
and do I imagine
their marching
feet ...

Sinistra ... diritto
Left ... right

Sinistra ... diritto
Left ... right
Sinistra ... diritto
Left ... ri ... gh ... ... t!

* * *

Tim the Nikon,
click, click,

and me ...
willing an audience
but stuck with a bloke and his dog
who defecates against a wheel,
not mine,
could have been Tim's,
he was too busy snapping to notice,

as Dave from Chester,
high viz, security,
shuffles back to the sanity of his cabin,

and
Tim from London,
on an assignment from the Old Law Courts in Wigan
as part of their
"The Road From Wigan Pier" exhibition
packs his camera away with an air of relief,
as I finally get to drive away,

and that evening,
Ar Sharon's car,
on our way to
Mr Ali's Indian restaurant in Middleton,
she was logging the music there,
happened to say

"Been anywhere nice?"

... Well,
brother the up to,
Dave the council,
incontinence the pads,
solar the lights,
Tim the Nikon,
Dave the security,
defecating the dog ...

as she
turns the radio up,
we arrive,

and Malik the waiter asks
"Been anywhere nice?"

... Well,
brother the up to,
Dave the council,
incontinence the pads,
solar the lights,
Tim the Nikon,
dog the defecating,
Dave the security,
Sharon the driver,

Malik the retreated
back into his kitchen
with an
"Excuse me,
mi poppadoms are done" ...
just a day in the life,
a life in a day,
a day and a life,

a passing moment of time
that'll provide a chuckle
as I sit in that high-backed chair
looking out of my window of memories
and reciting
"Ode to a turd"
as if a looped tape,

a tableau of stories
on the turntable
of mi mind
turning faster
and faster
and faster
and

fa ... s ... t ... ... e ... ... r

The Rain in Spain

falls mainly on ...
mi front window,

and mi sunburnt legs,
lived in pegs that've enjoyed
au naturelle and heatwaved
but now sadly wave the sun kaput
as arrive trench foot,

and I itch to ditch mi woolly warmers,
long pants abort,
dig out mi shorts,
sockless sandals flaunt with a determination
to taunt
varicose vein and
fungal nail infection,
dirty knees inspection
in spite of

73 years of sheltering behind the mask of
nocturnal wrinkle and
pimple and
dimple
of decorum

(excepting New Brighton Beach and a soggy woollen cossy
dragging a ridge in't sand and exposing mi tide mark)

as if in fright of sunlight
until ...
sod it,
peel off mi kit,

but only if the rain
falls on the sodding plain
in
Spain,

and not over №17.

*Time carries on but memories remain. I performed this in New
Brighton and at the very emotional end, a Liverpool supporter, he
draped mi shoulders with his Liverpool Football Club scarf ...
I felt humbled and proud to stand with them all ...
A 28 years' story of tragedy, of cover up, of truth.*

The Trip

This sleepy, in and out, Wigan township,
a list of expectant faces, receiving
another day, another trip,
our chariots of pleasure weaving

Worsley Hall for Lorraine,
a mind uncluttered of malice,
awaiting on Avenue Plane,
be transported to this television metropolis.

Marsh Green, Jeanette, iron steed,
trusty wheelchair oiled and ready,
electric ramp up, and she'd
picked her window seat already.

Worsley Hall again, Denise, eager smile
belies her curtain of death, ever present,
because diabetes, whilst waiting awhile,
in it's shadow it hangs, omnipresent.

And my Stephen, his epilepsy, they both
seize the day, banish dark thoughts,
today's the day we're loathe
afflictions to think of, abort.

Onwards we go, happy faces
these children of God, brave souls,

their good mornings and cheeky embraces
on this 15th of April, 1989, parallel goals.

Two buses full, route sorted, ensure
to our neighbouring capital city,
Granada Studios Tour
object of our propinquity.

East Lancs, foot down, excited chatter,
"is it time for our butties?" Tupperware packed,
Golborne, Leigh, speed limit not shatter
as mile upon mile they snacked.

City landscape veers to view,
this alien metropolis in the sky,
"Please Miss, I need the loo",
always one our patience to try,

pull over quick, wooded copse,
this wildlife haven of peace,
half the bus run, legs crossed,
that's better, what a relief,

back on, not long to go,
nearly there you lot, so quiet still,
here we are, Granada Tours Studio,
this way to the actors treadmill.

We sat in the Houses of Parliament,
and Downing Street, Number Ten,
we rambled about in wonderment,
and then we spotted Big Ben.

We went in the Rover's Return,
and Betty's Hotpot was good,
to the famous cobbles sojourn,

and the spot where Elsie Tanner stood,

her famous on-screen war
with Ena Sharples no less,
these ghosts of actors no more
in this palace of dreams process.

Early afternoon soon came around,
a good time was had by all,
passing Swinton, whilst homeward bound,
radio newsflash, F.A. Cup semi-final, football,

Liverpool versus Nottingham Forest at Hillsborough,
the game was stopped at 6 minutes past 3,
96 Liverpool fans died and 766 were injured
in the Leppings Lane Stand.
It is the worst stadium related disaster in British history,
it is one of the world's worst football disasters.

A lot of the people on the trip from the Pemberton Phab
(physically handicapped and able bodied) Club, including my
wife Alwyn and son Stephen, have since passed away,

but all their memories live on,
particularly through the never-ending quest
to find out the truth about how Hillsborough happened.

Granada Studios Tour re-opened temporarily,
now shut down once again
except in my remember.

So that trip on our memory imprinted,
same as the other trip, parents and wives,
and after years of reports reprinted,
it's a microcosm of all our lives.

And that trip, a long time ago,
we shared with another event,
terrible news coming through on the radio,
when Granada Studios Tour ... we went.

And
can I quote
press,
politicians,
police,
who pissed on the candle of justice,

and the people of Liverpool,

who carried a torch of truth
to relight it,

and to hear a statement
from our Mother Parliament,

"rotten to the core"

aimed at the South Yorkshire Police,
is a testament to the 28 years of struggle
to finally shout out the truth that

96 Liverpool fans were
killed unlawfully,
and,
776 Liverpool fans were
injured unlawfully,

Criminal prosecution charges proceeding:

David Duckenfield, Match Commander –
95 offences of gross negligence manslaughter.

Sir Norman Bettison, ex Merseyside Chief Constable –
four charges of misconduct in a public office. (Lying)

Graham Mackrell, ex Sheffield Wednesday Safety Officer –
health and safety charges.

Peter Metcalfe, solicitor for South Yorkshire Police –
perverting the course of justice by
helping to amend police statements.

Ex Chief Superintendent Donald Denton –
perverting the course of justice.

Ex Detective Chief Inspector Alan Foster –
perverting the course of justice.

and Liverpool football fans,
I hope you'll "NEVER WALK ALONE" ever again.

Dedicated to the Pemberton Phab Club
and the Hillsborough Family Support Group.

Mi last piece of Petya's vegan birthday cake,
73 years young and contemplate ...

When Did I Become Old?

Funny how we remember the traumas
of life,
like the first time I waited in a shop doorway
on mi first date,
and waited
and waited
and
that cruel moment of lost innocence when I realised
she's not coming,
and how long should we wait,
was there ever a scientific figure
or
does our optimism vary
from adolescent
to
pensioner,

how long would I wait now in that pie shop doorway
before taking regulation carnation out of mi lapel
and slinking into anonymity?

12 months to mi next Birthday
is perhaps pushing mi optimism a bit far
but
I'll try mi best,
If only for another slice of
vegan birthday cake.

N.I.C.E.

I've got mi bus pass,

                                aren't I ... lucky?

I can forget your name,

                              aren't I ... excused?
                                 (It's mi age.)

I can forget my name,

                              aren't I ... I forget?

I can have a lie-in every morning,

                              aren't I ... lazy?

I can tell a poem about a flatulence problem,

                         aren't I ... mischievous?

I've got mi old-age pension ... for life,

                                am I ... lucky?

I can get meals-on-wheels,

                              aren't I ... greedy?

I can deposit half of it down't front of mi shirt,

                            aren't I ... wasteful?

I can have a door opened for me,

                          aren't I ... privileged?

I'm usually offered a seat on the bus,

                              if I'm ... lucky.

I can wake up every hour for a piss,

                              not so ... lucky.

I've got Age-UK lady to cut mi toenails,

                          aren't I ... dependent?

I got ripped out of £30 with gutter cowboys,

                            aren't I ... trusting?

I get concessionary prices everywhere,

                            aren't I ... cheeky?

I get free eye tests and prescriptions,

                  aren't I a ... drain on th'economy?

I'm living too long,

                        aren't I ... inconsiderate?

I can drive along at 23 mph
with a long line of cars behind me,
                    aren't I a ... doddering old fart?
I can get mi biscuit tin from under mi bed
and count mi money,
                            aren't I... sad?
Funerals are becoming more regular,
                        aren't I ... nervous?
I can sit at home surrounded by mi memories,
                        I do ... and often.

I can ... give up,
tempting ... sometimes.

I can ... become invisible,
will I? ... Bollocks!!

    Cause I ... can still vote,
            can still protest,
                can stay out late,
                    can bring out this book,
                can lose mi teeth,
                can forget whether it's Tuesday
        ... or October,

        can learn to live again
            after a sequence of family tragedies
                left me alone,
                    and lonely,
                        and
                            just existing.

            I've got something to say,
            I've got someone to listen,

did I mention …   winter fuel allowance,
elderly persons railcard,
nursing home,
S.D.A.,
D.L.A.,
A.A.,
R.A.C.,
B.B.C.,
N.I.C.E?

The National Institute for Health and Care Excellence
have released the following statement:

"Wider societal impact" to be considered when deciding
whether a drug is approved,
particularly for elderly patients."

So if I get cancer … tough shit!

But I've got mi bus pass,

Am I …

lucky?

Val, an agency nurse new to the area, was on her way to see to the needs of a young man who has special needs and lives a few doors down from me.

Mi Doorbell

Lethargic,
early morning bog-eyed,
coffee,
didn't sleep very well
thinking
about things
that cling,
touching
a void,

blinking
back sleep,

mi pen unprepared
write and word,

"ping-pong-ding-dong"
doorbell,

"Hello,
does J???? live here please?"

Me:
"Er, no."

"I'm very sorry to disturb you,
I'll ring th'office."

"Er, no,
I'd like to show
where you go.

Let me see,
just let me walk to mi gate,
one, two, three,

four
houses,
white car,
not far,
that's where you want."

Excuse mi bare legs
as mi dressing gown barely
fights off the Wigan ... rain
as it caresses
mi inadequately
covered
brain.

We shook hands,
a pensioner
in his thin dressing gown,
varicose veined
naked legs,

and Val,
a nurse,
who begs
the question,
"Does J???? live here?"

We exchanged names
at a wet gatepost
in a quiet
suburban
street

where even the birds
were taking cover

and the nocturnal snails,
the stragglers,
beat

a slimy way home
to safety
and dry

which is what
Th'Owd Chap
did

as I waved goodbye

to

"a ding and a dong"
and mi early morning
passer-by,

mi early morning ...
story.

So mi blank day has started
with a ding
and a dong,
a snail ...
and a tale

of a chance
encounter

after a night of
counting sheep
still managed to keep
me awake.

Writers, eh?

RL Challenge Cup Final 2017, Wembley
Wigan v Hull

And I remember games past,
the excitement building up for weeks,
rosettes and wigs and scarves and
match tickets propped in full view of visitors
like a badge of honour,
'til
Friday,
butties and drinks and crisps and KitKats and
father and son,
evening express bus from Wigan bus station
seems to take forever as it ambles from city to town
disgorging and picking up
yawning commuters
as we stutter a kind of sleep in between
our adventure.

Buckingham Palace at 6.30 on this special
Saturday morning,
will the queen be up
shovelling her Rice Krispies,
silver spooned laden,
into her royal gob
and dribbling half of it down her nightie
and onto the head of her favourite Corgi,
two innocents from "up North" where we class royalty as
"our team"
that we were born into,
same as the other lot are born into
Gordonstoun
and
Eton
and
some such rubbish.

Still,
we stare outside the palace gates in wonder at
the pomp and history,
a million miles from our back streets
and grime
and simple
and humour
and passion for
not just a game
but
"The Game",

The Rugby League Challenge Cup Final
at Wembley,
that day arrived
in two Northern towns
to disgorge half of its occupants
via charabanc and train and car
and pony and trap if needs be
down to the capital
to cheer on
"our team".

I await this afternoon's battle
between
Wigan and Hull,
just me this time,
not outside
Buckingham Palace
so can someone tell her majesty
not to bother inviting me in
for a kipper butty,

an elderly gentleman
with his memories
of Wembley's past,
I shall dig mi cherry and white rosette out

and make a cup of tea in a cardboard cup
and
stand up for
"Abide With Me"
and sit down for
the "National Anthem"
and feel every tackle
and shout at the ref
and hopefully
applaud a valiant Hull performance
whilst cheering a magnificent
Wigan win,

all from the safety of
mi front room,
thanks to this new thingy called
television.
Good luck Wigan ...

Wigan lost to Hull.
The team return to Wigan the next day
to a subdued fans reception.

Wembley Return

The homecoming today
could be like drinking champagne
at a favourite uncle's funeral ...

as we smile through teardropped teeth
and go through the motions of
still loving our fallen heroes
whilst secretly
wanting to shuffle away
to an early tea,

and putting on a DVD of
past Wembley glory
whilst locking the dog in a spare bedroom,

and
packing the wife off to bingo,

then St. Helens at Langtree Park,
next game on't fixture, hoves into view
like a recurring nightmare,
and we decide to stay ...

if
only
to
prove
our
loyalty.

Hard lines Wigan,
life can be a series of
down,
and down again,
brush yesterday to one side
and remember ...

if life was without challenge
we'd get bored,
so
onwards to the Grand Final at Old Trafford
and
let's share the disappointments
and
the triumphs.

Keep smiling,
mine's a pint
and think on,

we still love you,

and an Owd Chap remembers
Wigan v St. Helens at Murrayfield,
2002,
not for the result,
some we win,
some we lose,
but because it was the last big game
that a dad and his son,

we were able to share together.

*Ar Sharon took me to watch it on't big screen at
St. Jude's Rugby League Club.*

*I stood up for 'Abide with Me',
and remained seated of course
for the 'National Anthem'.*

An elderly couple spotted holding hands
as they slowly walk away from ...

St. Helens and Knowsley Teaching Hospital

Fingers interlocking a
together journey
through life,
elderly man and perhaps
his wife,

as
a hospital appointment shared
and halving the pain of
bad news heard,

or
sick friend
locked into the rhythm of
ward and nurse and bedpan,
to visit and chat and reassure
as they
now wend

together feet
back to
matching high backed chairs,
pot of tea
and
Coronation Street.

I was privileged to hear Jeremy Corbyn speak in Liverpool,
and I quote him:

"Austerity is a political choice,
not an economic necessity."

This was driven home the day before
as I walked round Manchester.

People,
not all of them begging,
just living,
sleeping,
on the street,
in a doorway,

not looking,
not seeing,
not troubling anyone,
except perhaps
our conscience,

not existing ...
if we don't bother to look,

or ...
look without seeing.

Sunday Afternoon in a Sunny July Manchester

Looking through the window of Costa Coffee,
savouring a pot of tea for one,
soya milk,
£1.85,
and watching ...

People,
Where are they going?
Where have they come from?

Pink back-pack matching pink haired young lady
with a busy gait,
strides against the flow of conformity
and
Harvey Nichols
(look where I've been)
shopping ... bags,
as she cocks a snook
at designer frittery.

Pushchairs and prams and mountain bikes
shake along the cobbled ambience
of Market Street
as they pass the immobile
Jehovah's Witnesses
reaching out with their tracts
of wisdom,
and their solution to
world salvation,
or domination,
depending on which end of their arm
we pause at,
or speed by,
glanceless.

Children clutch parents,
who ignore magic bubble hawkers,
and jumping toy dogs,
and plastic swords,

and a street person
slumped against a bedecked window

of unbuyable goods.

Let's pretend they're not there ...
and they won't be.

All nationalities,
this passport to a free market,
all ages,
this ageless floe of humanity,
with the odd dog
looking in vain for a
tree,
or lamp post,
or a homeless leg stretched out
as if at home,
which they are,
we're just too busy to notice
or,
too embarrassed
or,
too guilty.

A window to this world,
looking out
from a pot of tea for one,
with soya milk,
in
Costa Coffee,
£1.85,
bottom of Market Street in Manchester,
a sunny last Sunday in July
when even the calendar stood still
on this snapshot
of
normality,
a normal Sunday,

even for that
homeless person
slumped against that overpriced
and
overstocked window of consumable,

so near yet
so far
from his
outstretched ...

despair.

If you've got it,
flaunt it,
and if you can't remember it,
take up gardening.
Age is only a wrinkle away from ... sod it,
on ...

World Naked Gardening Day
(Saturday 6th May 2017)

Foliage neatly coiffed fore and aft,
sensible location, well away from nettles
and wasp
and a fat blackbird looking for worms,

dibber polished to a proud sheen
and perhaps sporting a sponsor,
I'm open to offers
but
Palethorpe's Sausages,
perhaps not ... this time,

so,
Saturday the day, neighbours away,
dibber in hand to dunk,
hoping for sun and no frost I pray,
don't want it end up shrunk.

"Your honour ... I was just inspecting mi marrow."

I shall be weeding with the slogan:

"You're never too old,
too wrinkled, too cold,
join me ... be bold,

break out of that mould,
discard your blindfold,
a naked, proud threshold
and
dangle loose your marigold,"

and your hollyhock,
and force your rhubarb ...

the British weather ...
a cold front and mi tulip
will snap in on itself,
so,
a wing and a prayer,
a winkle and a pinkle,
I'll see you all there,
mi garden, forsooth, a tinkle.

I've got
nettle rash,
nappy rash,
chapped lips,
frosty sprouts
and a shrivelled Osteospermum,

I've discovered that secateurs are
best used with an upwards bias,

don't apply
'feed 'n' weed' in a breeze
and
sweet peas are prone to a cold front

and the garden bench
leaves ridges
on mi arse,

not a nice impression when stooping
and inspecting mi celery,

but,
sun on mi back
and
inhibitions a lack
and
well on mi way to
a gardening day
with attitude
but without clothes ...
if that nursing home doesn't
catch up with me first,
security hired,
well ...

Big Gladys from round the corner
who spies a chance to further her education,
she never married,

and an Owd Chap proving ...
who needs tattoos
with a body like mine,

until finally,

life catches up with nature,

does he have the accoutrements?
Or,
will it be a damp squib
as he waters his marrow ...
prunes his gardenia ... and,

poses amongst his sprouts ... and peas.

A cold and cloudy
№17
promises to illuminate nature in the raw,
that's lain dormant all winter
and Ar Sharon's photoshoot from back
to front
to side
garden
that'll go down in the annals as ...

bonkers,
but my age, who cares ...

and
mi underused trappings of age now on a
downwards trajectory,
clutch mi modesty
and
venture forth and discard
what I wasn't born with,
proving baldness is only a mind game

and skin
is for keeping things in
except when they insist on
gravity.
An unashamed whisper, fresh air,
encountering pink and wrinkled skin,
lifts a quivering tussock of hair
dangling loose mi garden therein.

Mi hollyhock, proud and erect,
rhubarb, heavenward force,
and dibber in hand, I inspect
damp patch, flower bed source

as unclothed and taken short,
water mi seedlings, I will,
waste not, want not as taught
and too idle, watering can fill

as today, World Naked Gardening Day,
Th'Owd Chap, inhibitions get rid,
whilst the sun shines, make hay,
and hope prying eyes well hid,

because horror, through window peep,
and shock, nuddy gardener unleash
the proverb, what you sow reap,
might end up
garden
display
centre-piece.

Motto:

"He stands amongst his cabbages, and peas"

... might make a suitable requiem when
I join that allotment in the sky,

and the question
dangling in the wind ...

did he
or
didn't he?

Big Gladys,
never been married but up for it,
a tremble in her legs
and a glint in her eyes,

and Ar Sharon waiting for that elusive flash,

as an icy blast sweeps round
the Trossachs
and wobbles mi pansies.

Is gardening all it's cracked out to be?
Can rhubarb be forced?
Has that nursing home still got a spare place?
Proving that
age
is only a wrinkle away from
sod it,
I might as well enjoy what I've got left
before mi guarantee runs out.

Did mi marrow come out unscathed?
Are peonies all they're made out to be?
Was Big Gladys's hot flush an aversion to cucumber?
Did I bare for a dare
or care,
even if mi geranium showed
a sign of overwatering?

Did I strip,
as I gripped and snipped mi
'past-its-prime'
but swaying in
a gentle breeze
pink carnation?

Did mi wrinkle sprinkle
as I tinkled
au naturelle
and no hands
and

a figure of eight
pattern?

Posing and
pouting and
potting and
picking
blackfly
off mi cheeks,
it's nice to sit,
dulcet
innocence of age
writing another page
of life,

cuppa in situ
to hide life's inadequacies,
dibber safely tucked away,
where
a cool night air
wafts through the slats
in't bench
and
frosts mi ardour,

ponder the
sneak ... peak
of a snapshot
that got
an army of question marks
to hark ...
no, he won't

but,
red rag to a bull
and long-johns (wool)

discard,
an innocent story,
the gory
remaining just a tantalising peek away
as I sway
this way,
that way,
any way ...
with legs crossed
and abandon tossed
to the night air ...

safe from the
threat of gun and
bomb and
behead and
gas,

and mass
exodus of family,

of children
fleeing terror
and homeless
and hate,

where fate ...
arrive at a world
that doesn't care,
and where
they lose their innocence.

Food kitchen
and lack of hope,
and cope
surrounded by an

unreachable land of plenty
whilst tables empty
of future.

Keep smiling,
keep caring,
keep gardening
and
keep daring
to
eavesdrop on the simple life,
an Owd Chap
as he
careers past his
three score and ten
with a gentle
two-fingered salute at the clock's tick.

Keep saying "NO to fox-hunting",
treat animals and birds
and all living creatures
as we would wish to be treated.

We've had a nice journey
pruning and
mooning and
weeding and
leading you along life's naked pathway,

thank you for
sharing mi rhubarb,
mi hollyhock,
mi clock
still ticking
albeit a little slower,
and

mi wrinkles
sneer and jeer and career
towards the night air
with
a fanfare of ...

"keep moving forwards,
one moment life's shit
then a bit less sad
and I'm glad
I hung in during those black days."

Thank you Ar Sharon,
Creative Director and
Horticultural Choreographer,
Fairy Stunt Co-ordinator
and Special FX Artist
who wanders about
as if in trauma
of
the camera viewfinder
and has gone off sprouts,

as he stands once again
amongst his cabbages ... and peas,

the answer to the shouted question ...
will he?

Yes ... I did.

Naked and proud,
just an
Owd Chap,
hoping to leave the world a better place,
a more peaceful place,

a more equal place,
a happier place

than the one I was born into,
a Second World War
of horror
and greed
and need
for a sharing of love.

Keep smiling,
keep gardening and
keep your clothes on

or, keep a potted plant handy
to hide your blushes.

Buttons keeps an eye on mi spelling.

Do you want these filing, Grandad?
'A Feline Trilogy', p.45

Ben Flower and Dom Manfredi surprise me.
'RL Challenge Cup Final 2017', p.92

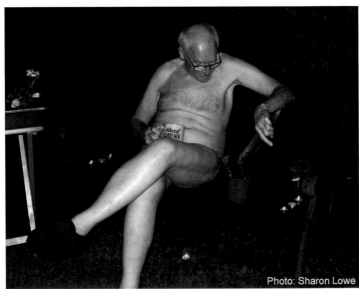

Mi Osteospermum (Daisybush) retreated in the cold.
'World Naked Gardening Day', p.102

Life doesn't need to be complicated.
'Beauty is ...', p.147

I, George Melling, with Ken Loach at Wigan Diggers' Festival 2016.
'McDonald's, Mi Mate Michael and Leonie', p.52

Photo: Sharon Lowe

I know mi place.

Meteor Showers

I sat outside, with the noise of the night,
through twilight, full darkness became,
as entertained, passing bats in flight,
I waited, visiting meteors, aflame.

Predicted shower of streaks of fire,
I heavenward squint and hope,
reflect on the vista atop me inspire,
and without the aid, telescope,

as darker and darker, before me transpire,
this not empty universe above,
of star and mystery and forever admire,
meaning of life ...

our tragedies ...

and love.

Beehive Mill №2 and Horrocks's Mill
(Glimpsed through the train window, Manchester side of Bolton.)

Bolton station, its environs
just,
stand two mighty emblems
downcast,
Horrocks's Mill, devoid
cotton dust,
Beehive Mill №2,
weavers past.

Two colossus of spinning
and cloth,
stand forlorn, sentinel,
and survey
mill hooter silent,
history both,

just memories of ...

cotton ...

and ... decay.

14 years ago since Stephen, our only son, passed away
whilst on holiday with us in Blackpool.
9 years ago since mi wife, Alwyn, passed away.
Today, Mothers' Day, I went in search of shadows, on't train to Blackpool.

Mothers' Day ... Revisited

Blackpool, the scene of mi past,
last glimpse of lost family, complete,
14 years rolled into today,
and maybe, mi memories I'll meet

as I stroll down the prom, seaside,
images of times long fade,
Th'Owd Chap, now on his own,
are resurrected in each step made

on his journey, this Mother's Day,
of poignant and sad and somehow
his life, he plodders along,
until his past and his future, like now,

meet on his promenade stroll,
with a greeting of remember, in spite
years of separation travelled between,
then homeward bound
as Mothers' Day
turns into ...
night.

I met mi memories,
but once again left them behind ...
in Blackpool.

Mid-October on a Still Dark 7 O'clock Saturday Morning

Buttons came down with me, had a pull of mi carpet and a bit
of brekky, a sit in't front window 'til boredom threshold sent her
back to bed to leave me to a quiet time of reflection ...

Life revolves round routine, the simple actions of day to day,
now and again such as holiday a break of the chain, or my
performance adventures, but mostly we've got a calendar, a
breakdown.

I'll have mi second cup of proper coffee shortly, a bite to eat
then get ready for a pensioner's day spread out as if important,
which it is to me but on paper a tad grey ...

Tilly, Milly and Ginger will be lined up outside with their
breakfast bowls and begging eyes, "please grandad,
miaowww", after which, "oh go on, just a little play".

The familiar of contentment which I lost big time seems just
yesterday sometimes and other times seems forever ...

Ey up, Buttons is down again coaxing a cessation of mi words
and a "hello, do you want a biscuit".
She purrs an "about time" as I'm once again back to mi thoughts
on this quiet time of day.
A few light streaks in a dismal sky promises perhaps rain to
welcome another weekend that, to be honest, retired, becomes
just another day that I'll cross off mi calendar to tell me when
Monday morning arrives as one month spreads into the next into
another year into another life to replace that which was lost ...

Just the gentle rhythm of a simple life ...
the gentle rhythm of words
to balance and steady an old man's musings ...

It's what we do ...

we remember another weekend
a long time ago
that seems like
yesterday.

6 Foot Conifer Hedge – First Cut of the Year

God,
cutting mi hedges
gets
harder
and harder.

I'll not say I'm old,
but I'm old,
mi arms are old,
mi legs are old,
mi ladder's old.   Ahhh, the pain of age.

Mi electric trimmer is new,
mi leaves and branches
I've just cut are new,

mi aches 'n' pains
are reasonably new,

mi moaning's new.   Ahhh, the newness of age.

God,
mi back,
'n' mi arms,
mi neck,
mi shoulder,
mi legs,

only thing that's not hurting
mi arse,
thanks to Sudocrem.

What?
I can't say that?

Well I did, it's mi age.   Ahhh, the anger of age.

Wisdom,
relax,
free prescriptions,
sod the alarm clock,
daytime TV,
Jeremy Kyle, Antiques Roadshow
Fiery Jack,
walking stick,
memory, (lack of).   Ahhh, the slowing down of age.

One step ahead of the nursing home,
googling euthanasia,
using a cheque book.   Ahhh, the dignity of age.

But,
I've got mi bus pass,
trouble is,
I can't sodding move to use it.   Ahhh, the futility of age.

But I can write about mi life.   Ahhh, the honesty of age.

It's not so bad really.   Ahhh, the acceptance of age.

So,
enjoy life whilst you're young.   Ahhh, the charity of age.

Now,
where did I put mi teeth?   Ahhh, I rest mi case!

A simple walk turns into an adventure and a story, a true story.

A Breath of Fresh Air

My age, mi grating joints
and lungs like an overused sponge
try to, whenever, a country walk,
so t'other day, took the plunge

to the hills my trusty steed,
well, to mi Micra I spoke,
as Wigan, out of we steered,
my aim, get away from folk.

It's good, own company enjoy
now and again, daily worries escape,
breathe in pure mountain air
whilst traversing God-given landscape.

Rivington village reached with rain
provokes mi wet gear wear,
best foot forward, onward and up
this green lichen, rocky thoroughfare,

breathe in and out at a rasp
mountainous incline traverse,
shitting hell, I'm getting old
as me and the sheep ... (baa), converse,

when out of the low lying clouds
half dog ... (woof), half donkey ... (hee haw), appears,
sudden movement I'll not make
unless in't th'air, springs its ears.

Luckily, slobbering greeting its aim

as back up the path it traversed
whereupon, looking up, I spotted
the chap it was with, who was versed

in saying his prayers, I thought
kneeled as he was by the edge,
and blessing the moorland growth
on this path of my mountain ledge.

"Howdo," I said, in passing,
"just met your dog ..." (woof) "glad it's tame."
"Oh, hiya ," said he, raising up,
"hope she behaved, Lucy's her name.

"Can't help but ask," sayeth I,
"is it worms for fishing you're at?
You see, I've lived a simple life,
nothing stronger than a Woodbine I've begat."

"Magic mushrooms's the aim of mi quest,"
as his plastic tub, contents reveal.
"They like the pure elevated air,
this low hanging cloud I'm concealed,"

"I dry them off a few nights,
then boil them up in a pan,
a few muslin filters perform,
the resulting mixture, they'd ban,"

"if they could, this elixir of youth,
this working man's narcotic of escape
that grows wild and free in my hills,
unnoticed and unknown, magical landscape."

"Until now," I say. "Show me,
this tiny fungus, ribbed crown,

who'd have thought my walk today
meet this famous elixir of renown."

I was tempted, you know, we are,
even at my age a breaking of shackle,
instead of mi camomile tea
a "pot for one" brain rattle,

but I didn't, said mi goodbyes ... (ta-ra)
to this chap and his quest for his dream,
and Rivington Pike was conquered
lifting clouds and a magic sunbeam.

All downhill the rest of mi walk,
at this nirvana of peace, magic climb,
and without any stimulated assistance
another world was transported for a time.

So there you have it, my jaunt,
communing with nature that I keep,
three hours of God's mountain air,
just me,
and the fells,
and the
sheep ... (baa)

Mi elderly, disabled brother's wing backed fireside chair, the leg snapped off, and as he has to use a three wheeled Zimmer to move about, I had to somehow manoeuvre it outside for his safety, and I'm not in the first, or second, flush of youth, although I've got mi original joints, a rarity I'm told these days, but their guarantee's run out. Anyway, I rang the Council, was eighth in't queue, and patiently waited ... and waited ... and waited ... and wai— then a voice. Explained our predicament, was told it would cost £10. I quietly expressed surprise that we're being charged for NOT FLY TIPPING, a local councillor is in this week's Wigan Observer pointing at a pile of discarded furniture and expressing anger, and quite right, but now he wants to come and point his public spirited fingers at this now stranded chair ... because I expressed my willingness to pay the charge by debit card over the phone, whereupon the nice young ... she sounded ... a young voice anyway ... Lady asked ... "IS IT DRY?" ... I said, "It's been outside all night, has it been raining?" ... She said, "Yes, and the refuse chaps won't take any wet furniture ... so sorry ... and good luck." Well, I've got a Micra, it's ok for carrying a packet of socks, a loaf and a bag of sprouts, but it pulls its face at a chair, so the chair doesn't sit, cause it's leg is at a funny angle, so it tilts forlorn and unwanted outside looking in at what was once it's purpose in life. I'm only hoping that when I am ready for that furniture store in the sky, a bit of wet won't delay my disposal, because I fully intend to piss misself just to get mi own back!

A Chair, a Binman and Life

Mi brothers chair, high-backed,
and strong,
afraid the feet didn't last ...
that long.
T'other day he sat ...
the chair did tilt,
cause sodding leg developed
severe wilt ...

it broke.

Now ... this comfy, this sentinel ...
fireside,
is discarded, new home ...
outside.
Bin men await if
£10 get,
except ... won't collect,
if wet.

So, rejected, this chair
of distinction,
its purpose now become
extinction.
No use in'th'house
its job,
sits outside, an occasional
sob.

And this is life, plodder
along,
first flush of youth, and family,
strong,
until aged, and brittle,
and bent,
like this chair, our strength
now spent.

We await those binmen
in't sky,
an exorbitant fee and
if dry,
me and chair not be
outdone,
stick

£10
where
not
shine
the
sun.

*Our Louise picked it up today, and this faithful little wingback has
supported its last weary body, and sits, nay tilts, amidst the flotsam
and jetsam of discarded dreams, and if someone in the future would
care to silently lift its little cushion, there would be revealed its daily
secreting of dried peas, biscuit crumbs, and thirty seven pence in loose
change, together with a paracetamol and a used paper tissue,*

R.I.P. Wingy.

A curlew, a cafe, some caves, underground passageways, a walk with the Devil and John Ruskin , writer and critic friend of JMW Turner ... and cheesy chips ... just a normal Wednesday day out, this pensioner with attitude, a pen, a pad and another story to tell ... uneventful ... never ... that saw me once again, Quink refreshed barrel, heading for the fleshpots of Lancashire tinged with the stone of Yorkshire where even the sheep know their rights, the hills are more than mere pimply utterings ... and I shall once again take notes in the hope that I can paint another picture, not with watercolours like Turner, but an old head, a new imagination and a line of blue-blacked, fountain-penned words ... and just maybe ... a barm cake with mi cheesy chips ... And as I anticipate another measly Winter Fuel Allowance payment I reflect that writing doesn't yet carry VAT and sheep don't half leave a load of shit.

A Curlew, a Cave, and a Curve in the River Overlooked by the Devil

Th'Owd Chap, his place has found,
this Ingleton village of quaint,
soon White Scar Cave be bound,
sudden pangs of hunger brings faint,

shakily, Curlew Craft sojourn,
cafe within, welcome break,
veggie burger, pot of tea soon turn
mi starving to full with a cake.

So mi pot Earl Grey, loose leaf,
tea strainer, old-fashioned charm,
on sale artwork, Melling (Keith),
all surrounding mi chips, veggie barm.

And now White Scar, hilltop fog,
via Yorkshire Dales National Park,
upon arrival Stella, friendly dog,
black coated retriever without bark.

And we queue 'til next timed tour,
and anticipate ten pounds a time,
this adventure our latest newer,
and seize the day with rhyme.

Hard hat and Darren our guide,
set off, cave detour down below,
eighty minutes of fissure smooth side,
low roof, rushing torrent, pace slow.

Became intrepid explorer all,
as passed re-enactment, Christopher Long,
whose dream, these tunnels now enthral,
as we crouch, then crablike along.

Judge's Head, Devil's Tongue, The Squeeze,
these imprinted images we passed,
Big Bertha with sword of Damocles,
10,000 year old stalactites amassed.

And I'm spelled to mention the Witch,
various images of Nipple, Face, Hat,
fingers of stone with barely a twitch,
with her familiar, the Witch's Cat.

Crouching tunnel opens up spiritual vast,
water torrent and infinity explore,
mouth open in wonder and gasp,
this underground, cathedral-like awe.

Subterranean caves, water course worn,
over thousands of years to score,
provokes spasms of breaths indrawn,
each passageway we ramble, explore.

'Til daylight disgorge end of tour,
back to rhythm day in, day out,

natural wonder lives under this moor,
I discovered when out and about.

As ...
Kirby Lonsdale beckons, day's end,
of images to gather and store,
market town of passageway wend,
all leading to River Lune shore.

Devil's Bridge spans millennia of year,
down-river from Ruskin's View,
elevated from vista sheer,
in the shadow of ancient yew

stood sentinel, St. Mary's graveyard,
watch over all sleeping soul,
as twilight slowly shadows promenade,
reflect my afternoon as mole.

Deep below lonely Yorkshire Dale,
and now, falling leaves garland stroll,
as with pen recreate my tale,
of life, Th'Owd Chap, his peephole,

opportunity gifted, life back-end,
as alternative, cosy slipper and chair,
I write daily adventures wend,
and my reward ...
to humbly ...
share.

A Cut Above the Rest

First cut of the year,
grass waking from nature's winter slumber,
mi lawn,
to yawn
and stretch towards the sun
and the warmth of
a spring, bright afternoon,
long awaited
after what seemed
a passing of time
dormant and dark,
that embraced a stark
and mingy

'Winter Fuel Allowance'
off a Tory government
that promises,
then turncoats,
then floats ....
public criticism,

mi mingy
'Winter Fuel Allowance'
that warmed me until
the end of November,
just until, needs must,
hot water bottle,
long-john,
savings gone ... or at least diminished,
and extra socks
to slow down mi 'lectric bill,

a 'Winter Fuel Allowance'

off this apology of a political party
that I haven't got as Facebook friend
as I wend
mi path,
seasons of mi life
and seasons of mi shady back garden,
up a line,
down a line,
like a miniature Wembley Stadium
but minus the goal posts
and ghosts ...
of overpaid prima-donnas.

All part of nature,
write as I mow,
as I go,
each furrow a line of mi story,
writing pad perched on top of mi blue bin,
a Tory bin,
only because it was the cleanest
so no hidden meaning,
no slight leaning
away from mi roots,

you might just be able to pick up
I'm not a Tory supporter,
if I had the choice between
a dose of diarrhoea
or
the local conservative club's cheap beer,
I'd get a pack of bog rolls in.

As mi regular postman
delivers,
not a premium bond win
but a daily dose of Post Office junk,

unasked,
but he's tasked
as Royal Mail supplier,
advertising flyer,
another waste
of natural resource
placed,
or chucked with a tut of resign
into aforementioned recycling bin.

And professional as he is,
barely a blink
this story to go
as I mow
another chapter
that includes him,
he doesn't know ... until now.

Lifting of a green planter reveals,
and blinking in surprise at what is an
unearthly shattering of their
sleep,
a huddled heap
of woodlice,
scattering as if mass fight,
Wigan on a Saturday night.

I pause,
and lift a snail to safety,
its head emerging
from its shelled embrace,
antennae-ed face
studies me
as if to plea,
be gentle.
Why harm on purpose?

Ode to a Snail

Hello little snail, your own house
and your penchant for dark and wet,
and as I cut mi lawn, you still abed,
being careful, mower too near not get.

No bedroom tax worry your world,
nor protest for somewhere to live,
nor interest in Tory outpourings,
but you do like cucumber that I give.

Sometimes, when I've got some, wet night,
you'll wait there an orderly queue,
and I dispense your green treat slice by slice,
cause my garden, part of your life too.
There's Brian and Briony, the rest,
all mi mates, mi garden gang,
my bed time you get up en masse,
scoff your supper, the whole shebang.

In harmony, me and you, we share,
and my dahlias, so what, the odd chew?
We should all in this world, others respect,
each contribution, no matter how small, value.

* * *

Side garden of two seasons,
sun and shade,
up the line, down the line
until I hear it, like a yawn ... infectious
as another mower strikes up a melancholy,

a shattering of peace, an unleash
of bored pensioner,
so now there are two
competing.
Third and final front garden,
bathed in full sunshine,
up the line, down the line
tells me,
everything's going to be fine.
As I wonder each year,
and age does this,
will I be able to,
and if not, who will do
what we take for granted,
mow mi lawn, paint mi gate, fasten mi fly?
As I ... satisfy,
stand at mi blue bin,
fountain pen, book, and look
at mi job well done,
and write a story ...

First cut of the season
gives me a reason
for
getting out of bed.

Fatty Blackbird's Just Been

Fatty blackbird's just been,
he stretched,
said ... "Any chance of a top-up?"
and shat on the side of mi wall.

This is the minutiae of my world,
I shall have a seven week
'no-drone zone',
no listening to argument
and counter argument,
the price of ribbed condoms
and cornflakes
and birdseed
and free euthanasia for pensioners.

The nasty and venom
and lies and promise
and anger and despair,
and biased media.

Fatty blackbird's just flown back,
he stretched and shat on the other side of mi wall.

I tend to agree with him, it's Labour for us.
I like Jeremy,
I like his honesty,
I like his common sense approach to politics,
I like his caring approach to politics,
I like his quiet approach to politics,
I like Jeremy ....

I wonder why the blinkered,
the 'grab everything', the selfish,

I wonder why they deride him,
are they frightened of ... sharing ... of caring ... of daring?
To show an ounce of compassion
and a determination to spread our wealth
more evenly?
Are they frightened of looking outwards
from their own little ivory towers?

Me and fatty blackbird, we'll put the world to rights,
I wish he wouldn't keep shitting on mi wall though!

A New Day

What we've lost
it's gone,
except perhaps in memory.

What we've got
is now,
a new day,
a new chapter
as we turn that page
called age.

A new way
on life's sometimes rocky road
to be strode,
a winding highway
called life,

and I'm lucky,
not lucky to have lost,
but lucky to have had,
and yes, I'm sad ... but glad
of my time spent
with Stephen and Alwyn ...

Sometimes our happiness is only lent
until a calling back
promotes a black
cloud of despair.

I shall remember them today
as I wend my way
towards midnight
and a reunite

of times past,
but only in dream.

Moving forwards hard fought
whilst answers sought
to that question
we all seem to ask:

"Why me?"

What we've lost
it's gone,
except perhaps in memory.

What we've got
is now,
a new day,

until tomorrow.

Time moves on ...
but memory
remains
frozen
in
time.

I visited mi family grave, these thoughts crowded mi head.

A Piece of England
(A grave, a pot and a memory.)

Not just a mound of earth,
a plaque, a name,

an anonymous churchyard,
a lonely grave,

where tears nestle
amongst
a daily visit of
love, or duty,

where the past
visits our now,
and clings to
our future.

This is our destiny,
our plot of English heritage,
denied in life
but,
land-owner in death.

Kings of their castle,
this family in spirit,
no longer
hopefully,
to argue about
food on't table,
or money,

or worry
health
and
employment,

who visited this self-same
garden of memory,

in preparation
for
what they've
now
become.

Just a name,
on a plaque,
on a mound of earth.

JUST A MEMORY

What happened yesterday
is with us today,
and governs
our tomorrows.

I was asked to perform a guest spot in Huddersfield
and I wrote this piece especially,
to introduce me and try to explain
what it meant to be once again back in
this Yorkshire town after a 15 year absence ...

There was a distinct pause at one point ...

Poetry isn't just words on paper,
it can be a releasing of buried hurts,
a remembering of life as it used to be,

painful, raw emotion.

A Pilgrimage Revisited

Stephen mi son and
Alwyn mi wife
and me ...
we looked forwards
Wigan versus Huddersfield at
what was then the
John Smith's stadium,
cherry and white carefully worn
to signal a family of fans
weaving a pathway
towards the
M62 Rugby League corridor ...

And the biff and bash of
that days must win at all costs
gladiatorial battle ...

because of a
Red Rose and a White Rose,

Lancashire honour against a Yorkshire
who we once thought their
only claim to fame was
Betty's Tea Rooms ...
and
Harry Ramsden's fish and chips.

I must say I've been converted,
I must say ... because me and Ar Sharon
need to get out safely,
we come in peace,
and we'd rather *not* leave in pieces.

And Yorkshire tea,
an insipid substitute for
Lancashire tea,
strong brew of which is used
for degreasing ovens
and bathing pet ferrets
and ...

The M62 services
with its welcoming
Burger King for Stephen,
cuppa and a cream scone ... with jam, of course,
for us two

whilst we could nearly hear the not far now
Yorkshire sheep, and breathe in,
mingling with carbon and petrol and
cow shit ...

A fresh moorland air
to cleanse the Wigan smog,
until destination.

And ....
that was then, 15 years ago.

My lifetime ago,
my memory ago,
my sadness ago ...

Stephen died,
then Alwyn died
and our trips across the eagerly awaited
backbone of England became
a line on a map,

another of those memories that somehow,
in spite of the tears they cause,
we treasure.

I haven't been to Huddersfield for 15 years ...
and now,
writing and performing stories and poems ...
tonight there'll be a bridge of words,

and a memory of
me and Alwyn and Stephen ...
My first time back in Huddersfield
without them ...
a fifteen year journey of a new life,
unexpected beginnings...
and reinventing of hope.

every mile *is a memory.*

Mine   where
    is a winding   up the M62
            road

Beauty is ...

Beauty is ... watering mi garden,
and marvelling at the rainbow
sparkling in the fine mist.

Beauty is ... this Californian poppy
that speaks to me with colour.

Beauty is ... drawing mi curtains back,
and saying,
good morning ...
to my world,
and Buttons answering back ...

"Miaowww,
where's mi breakfast?"

Beauty is ... another Sunday
to reject,
as I'm coaxed back to a past memory,

or embrace,
as a going forward,
collecting a scrapbook ...

of wonder,
of nature,
of beauty,
of sunshine,

of my blueprint,
my calendar,
my lifeforce,
my destiny,

my ... ...

beautiful Sunday morning,

when even the birds,

mi extended family,

with fatty blackbird, their spokesman,

sing with an extra vibrato
as they squabble over
mi proffered seed,

and shit on mi picnic chair.

Beauty is ...

somewhere to live,
someone to share,
something to eat,
somehow to care,

for the army of
people,
families,

fleeing terror
and meeting cold hearts.

Beauty is ...
a warm welcome.

Beauty isn't ...
the hundreds of thousands
of people killed,
the hundreds of thousands
of people displaced,
countries left in the grip
of turmoil and terror

and
a legacy of lying and
misinformation
from politicians.

Beauty is ...
having the freedom and honesty
to strive for a
fairer society.

Beauty ... to this old man ... is today.

This old man sat alone, curtains open, the Pemberton night sky alight
with rockets and colour and noise ...
and, mi thoughts drifted back to Stephen
and how much he looked forwards to this day of ...

Bonfire Night

Childhood memories of Guy Fawkes,
and sparklers,
and fireworks,
and hot dogs,
and treacle toffee,
and wrap up well,
and family,
and excitement for weeks beforehand.

And burnt and black potatoes
straight out of the glowing embers
that seemed, to our young fingers,
to stay hot until next year ...

Bonfire night,

a dad's memory of torch,
box of matches,

carefully stored ...
then opened ...
selection box,

a muddy trudge to the end of the garden
and ignite,
to shrieks of ooohhhs ... if coloured lights,
or
aaahhhs ... if bangs or frights.

This ... particular year,
bonfire no longer burning,
fireworks just a flash of memory
this November the fifth,
now, I sit with mi curtains open
and watch a memory burning brightly once again,
in the night sky.

Me, and mi family together ... if only in dreams,
at our ...

Bonfire Night.

White flash,
almighty crash,
this tonight's bouquet
of a multi-coloured display

and,
I miss mi family,
a firework selection to sort,
of that box of tricks
carefully bought

Lights out ... blackout,
and sparklers ... hand out
to muffled up and rosy cheek,
and cry of joy and excited shriek,
and firework wick ... carefully light,
pent up force to ignite this ...

Bonfire Night.

Another memory,
another year longer,
emotions get stronger,

but still,

as I sit on mi own,
through mi window ... look,
all the memories unravel of mi unlocked scrapbook ...
Another year gone by
since final goodbye
on this ...

Bonfire Night,

and the stars ignite
mi emotions.

I miss mi family on this, November the fifth.

No longer to share
in the cold night air,

not now to relay
this Guy Fawkes' display,

treacle toffee to buy,
cups of Bovril to try,

dry night to wish
on this typically English
custom and charm,

and its Technicolor explode
on this life's sometimes rocky road.

Another year gone,
how many to go?
I sit by mi window
looking out at the glow,

the flashes and rockets
and bangers galore.

On this, my life path furrow,
another memory
to sparkle and fizzle and flare ...
then glare no more.

This is my new life now,
life moves on ...

It's just that
the sky doesn't burn as bright
on bonfire night,
it isn't the same, you see ... for me.

(DINNER TIME)

Oh,

I Do Like to Be Beside the Seaside,
I do like to be beside the ...

see
the sea,
the sand,
the shows

and rows and rows of
candy floss
across
and round
and found
intermingling with
hot dogs,
fried onions,
chips

and dips
in the sea
ever mindful of poo and wee,
product of waste management
a tad crap
at managing
and polluting our coast
except those that boast
a blue flag.

With exorbitant parking charge,
by and large
run down guest house
to espouse

hen party and stag do
who,
let's just say,
cavort
and shout
and mount
full frontal assault
on
family and values
and peace.

But each
to their own
as I moan and groan,
pensioner's prerogative
to offset meagre pension,

and did I mention
the rain in Spain
falls mainly on
sodding Southport and Blackpool
and a chill in Rhyl
from that big hill,
(Snowdon)
can permeate the woolliest of coss
with a loss
of libido and feeling
and a reeling
of
will to live.

Oh,
I do like to be beside the seaside,
I do like to be beside the ...

oh

sod it,
on second thoughts
I'll stay in
and prune mi
hollyhock
and force mi rhubarb.

(TEA TIME)

The rain in Spain fell mainly on
sodding Cleveleys,
a bloody monsoon
all afternoon
our misfortune,
we didn't follow mi advice,
we, the other half of, being Ar Sharon,
shall we have a ride while it's nice?
Entice ...
why not?

Persisted down all afternoon.
Still,
a trawl of charity shops,
in and out hops,
bargain or three,
then tea
in Cleveleys Kitchen
which included syrup sponge and custard,
that ruptured
mi top button,
it's costed in mi diet.

Sunshine and shower
and cower
in a dripping doorway,
candy floss and dross and a loss

of the will to live,
perfect beach just out of reach
and a sea
mixed with pee
and other unmentionables ...

We make do and mend, transcend
our shitty weather, whether
rain or fine we'll sing the line ...

"Oh, I do like to be beside the seaside,
I do like to be beside the ,,,"

if you think of it ...
just like life.

A sixty five year old memory,

a seven year old lad with
a drooping soggy cossy,
and ...

An 'Owd Chap
who
struggles to
remember yesterday.

I wrote this whilst on mi way to New Brighton,
I was due to perform at
The Poet Tree,
run by a young poet mate
Matt Delaney,

I started it whilst standing on a deserted
railway platform,
middle of nowhere,
unless you live near ...

Garswood Station

A platformed
peace
and
quiet,
occasional tweet and
change of tree
as a solitary sparrow sits,
sentinel perch,
fluffs its downy feathers,
shits,
and goes back to sleep

to dream about its
waking feed
and
next year's breeding season.

I stand,
and shuffle one leg north,
one leg south,
and mi head
arrivals bound
as I await ...

the 18.14
to Liverpool ...

A solitary 'Owd Chap
on his 65 year memory
of ...

sand castle,
one and six in pennies,
flannel shorts,
black pumps,
snotty nose,
and ...

an adventurer's excitement
of
the unknown.

An escape from
the embrace of Wigan
with its visiting
River Douglas
that to our young eyes
might be ...

the Amazon
or
the Nile
because
we'd never seen either,

and ...

Liverpool,
a city of tall building
and seagull,
first glimpse of the
River Mersey,
Royal Iris
that to innocent eyes
towered
like an ocean going
leviathan,

and sailed into the wind
of a battling
Irish Sea
until spied through binoculars,
the magical place,
discovered and conquered
by a child's eyes ...
New Brighton!

Where awaited a
soggy,
woollen
swimming costume
that rubbed a channel in't sand.

Bucket and spade,
a paddle beach

that swept to the other side
of my world,
my seven year old world.

Endless sun,
and colour,
and toffee rock,
and jam butties,
and pop
and crabs
and a holiday
that was
special,
a child's growing up
ago

that
65 years later
can't be re-created
because of
silting sand
and
lack of investment ...

But, I did meet ...

a "ferret cross the Mersey",
little Kalimo the pet ferret,
out for a 2nd birthday stroll
along the prom with
its dad Steve,
both of them legends of Birkenhead,

and sampled the delights of
a
veggie curry eatery,

and nearly sampled
the multi-flavoured scoops
of an ice cream parlour,
but,
the sodding place shut early!

And that was now,
t'other night,
but mi thoughts
from long ago,
I dredge
a little lad's memory
to
that grey time of
post-war years,
as he arrived at
New Brighton,

and discovered his utopia
of sun and sand
and sea ...

His Narnia with foreshore,

just like the other night really,
but minus the ferret,

and as mi woollen cossy
once again sags
on mi washing line
of memory.

And as I shrink into
my colouring book
of driftwood,
this little urchin

from the grey of
post-war Wigan,

once again,
65 years later,
breathes in
the endless ocean whisper
of a
world conquered,

life lived
becomes just a memory.

Same as today
will become a memory,

a homeward bound
back
to Garswood.

A sleeping sparrow

and

a
new horizon
*on my journey of
train

and boat

and pen
and perform,

and ... a little lad born again ...
65 years later.

When I'm but a pricked pimple on life's journey ...
I'll find, hopefully, the answer to the question(s) ...
are the Jehovah's Witnesses the only ones to go to Heaven,
if so, and they've all been saved, whose door will they sodding knock on?

Do They Use Three-Wheeled Walkers (Zimmers) in Heaven?

Upright it aids us become
when limbs, go slow, arrive,
ravages of age not succumb
as loosening of bones we strive.
This mobile "leg-up" on wheel,
attached bag all shiny and black,
speed along determined and zeal
marks well-worn path of tarmac,

Are pies healthy ...? And who cares?

And petrol, no need to buy,
M.O.T. and insurance unsold,
if the Olympics, an event qualify,
100 metres, Zimmer sprint, medal gold.

If I bequeath mi Wigan season ticket to a St. Helens supporter ...
will it please God?

This machine, our extension of life,
a mechanical equivalent thoroughbred,
providing lift in time of strife,
I've ordered mine in red.
Do they use Zimmers in Heaven?

National Poetry Day 2017

Poetry
enables me to
talk about
the mad and
bad and

sad,
that moment of life's trauma
locked into mi heart
and released years later
drip by drip
as word
to be heard
by anyone who'll listen.

Sometimes a tad
daft
as we forced mi rhubarb and laughed
and
weighed mi melon
whilst photographed
in *flagrante delicto*,
(bare-arsed for Naked Gardening Day),

or
hang onto the memory
of innocence
and tragedy
and avoidable ...
save for the profit of indifference,

the sound of excited young feet

pattering downstairs

as the sky
slowly wakes up
on their school day morning.

Toast
or rice pops
or eggy soldiers,
today's only question
to tax an otherwise
perfectly
ordinary day,

as,
satchels
and dinner money
and hasty goodbyes ...
"see you tonight mum",
and a skip
and a jump
and excited chatter
through the school gates
on this breaking day.

51 years ago,
when a hundred and sixteen children
never retraced their
journey home,

and
28 adults,
in an instant
of black spoil heap,
were smothered in
a nothingness
of
National Coal Board
Indifference.

And
a
giant
wet
sliding
nightmare
of
discarded
lives.

Aberfan
21st October, 1966.

Today
a verse or two
to while away mi time,
circumstance and life anew
this gentleman of rhyme,

as four walls a prison became,
unexpected traumas in life
when happiness not guaranteed remain,
first mi son and then mi wife,

their passing, a lasting gift
'til poetry, my safety release,
a sudden, welcome lift
brought my life a kind of peace.

'Til today, National Poetry Day,
to read, enjoy or write,
and I just wanted to say,
with words we can excite ...

and unite.

Put a Sock In It

Mi good mate, she lost her partner,
life's like that, we go sailing along then ... wham!
I'm so sorry, my thoughts are ever towards,
but,
the trauma of losing a loved one continues
well after a funeral.
That period when tears have temporarily dried up
to be replaced by an aching heart,
the clearing and throwing and giving
all those no longer needed
clothes and artefacts
and memories
that were important
in day-to-day living ...

These in this bag for charity,
those in that bag for dumping ...

And I was asking her was she coping ok?
and she said ...
"You know, George, he had 63 pairs of socks."

And now I'm wondering,
and I've no thoughts
of celestial journey
at this minute
feel assured.
I've only just got mi passport
and I had a new outside light fitted yesterday
but, mi thought processes,
that grey matter with defective memory valve
but still able to weave a tale or two,
I'm convulsed to go on a counting spree,

itemise that what keeps mi going
from one bag of crisps to a multipack ...

So book and pen to hand,
and I might leave the completed list with mi will
so individual hand wringers
can anticipate a pair of
off white underpants
and tartan golfing socks,
(they were 5 in a pack
and cheap).

3 combs, not recently used;

thermal tights and vest (rugby in February freezes mi cockles off);

boxer shorts(including a Christmas pair complete with
Rudolph carrot nose bulging a prominent spot
eliciting nudge nudge wink wink);

a 1953 Coronation penknife;

books – numerous;

Cosyfeet slippers – one pair;
mi John Collier wedding suit;
sunflower seed heads ... gone black;

more books;

tin of hardened paint (admired when first applied);
washers; nails; bits o' string;
Polyfilla with a brick like consistency;

and yet more tossing books;

can of WD40 (last resort after a prayer and a swear);
stamp album; collection of cig packets and old maps
that still show Rutland, Cumberland and Mercia;
and Wigan, a stronghold of the Roman Empire,
(at least on Saturday night in King Street);
a dolly blue;
tin of Fiery Jack;
and glass washboard!

I'll be glad it's not me who
has to sort it all out.
I might leave mi body to science ...
except for mi feet,

I've got a sodding drawerful of socks!

Goodbye ...

Block WS 6
Row A
Seats 164 163 162

Me, Alwyn and Stephen
enjoying together
the crunch and speed
and need
for a win,

or lose.
perhaps a draw?
Drop goal seeker
and
occasional streaker,
skydiver to soar
and fireworks
and more
until
kick off,

then the
"gerrum onside",
the
"come on, ref",
the
"dirty swine"
and game end
bereft
or hooray
depending on who won.

The rugby friends and

cheery hellos,
the
"come on Wigan"
and plaintive
"oh nos"
as the other lot scores.

Alwyn terrified being hit,
here comes the ball,
"oh shit!"

Until season 2002,
Block WS6
Row A
Seats 164 - 163

We went in sadness
but
Seat 162 whispered an empty hello
as Stephen's memory guards the South Stand pitch ...
which
puts the rugby into perspective,
at least until season 2007.

A pity
but
in life,

there's no referee
to wave a yellow
or
a red
card,

mi wife, her seat 163
no longer needed.

Seat 164 remained empty
week after
week after
grief
after month
until a tentative walk down the stair
to an empty chair
sighing
a tearful greeting
as if meeting
a ghost.

Until this afternoon
I'll fight
back a tear
or two or three
remembering the year upon year
as I,
memory impaired
and February, March and April dared ...
Summer rugby indeed
as the cold
takes hold
an Old Chap getting soft
and he'll doff
his cap
at game's end
and wend
his way home
alone,

for his last time,
perhaps.

A seven year old boy
being lifted into the Lad's Pen

at Central Park ...
slowly drifting towards the
East Stand car park

to place his spent season ticket
into
that box of memory
that forms a lifetime.

It would be nice if
Wigan
could win,

just for me, and Alwyn, and Stephen.

Mi son, Stephen, died in 2002 leaving seat A162 empty.
Mi wife, Alwyn, died in 2007 leaving seat A163 empty.
Come 5pm tonight seat A164 will be empty
as an old man
says goodnight to Malcolm on the gate
and walks a lonely path away from his
memories.

dependable, patient, wise,
racing paper, fag, and dodgy knee.

I settled down, family, kid,
now he's a great-grandad, start again,
with 'is football, un 'is Woodbine, un 'is ash,

his fishing un rugby, ever there,
this always mi mate, mi grandad,
un 'is ever-full pocket o'cash.

Grandad un me, a team,

pity it's only a dream,

because he went to war before I was born.

They never found his body.

He's still lying somewhere in a now-healed field in France.

Lost, but not forgotten.

And if you applaud,
you're not only applauding me
but mi grandad,
and all the other grandads,

and dads,
and sons,
and husbands,
and brothers,
and uncles,
and partners,
and pals ...

who never came back

all those years ago.

Look for his name, mi grandad,
on Wigan War Memorial.

I still go there sometimes, un sit,
un hold his hand,
un I swear,
'is Woodbine ash ...
still floats down on mi 'ead.

George Melling is a masterful weaver of words. He writes with soulful heart. He writes with beautiful honesty. He writes with wonderfully wry humour. His poetry is so richly layered and his performances are cheeky and charming. In the space of one poem he'll have you laughing until your sides hurt, nodding in agreement at his insightful observations about the world, and wiping away tears at his reflections on love and loss. His words paint powerful poetic pictures, with images that stay in mind long after his performances.

Rose Condo
Writer, Performer & Poet

Suspend your pre-conceived ideas about old Northern men, this Owd Chap smashes it with a smorgasbord of poetic storytelling – expect wry wit, heart-break and protest. An absolute treat.

Louise Fazackerley
Poet & Theatre-maker

Clasped tightly within the bosom of his poetry family, George Melling has blossomed as a poet, a performer, an actor, and a scribe of enormous gentleness and subtlety. Without warning, he can pull the rug from under a room full of people, lulled by his homely, quotidian observations, only to be reminded of how brief and sudden, how precious and vicious human life and death can be. He possesses a deft touch with understated humour, and his warmth and generosity of spirit shine through in this collection.

It's impossible not to love George and his poetry, and I defy anyone to make it through Th'Owd Chap's book with a dry eye.

Laura Taylor
Poet & Performer

George first came along to one of our drama courses with no experience in acting, and, to say the very least, he was apprehensive. He had no confidence in his own ability or the ability to learn lines, doubting his own memory, which, through his own determination, improved considerably over the project and performances. However, he brought along with him the most important elements when embarking on a new journey; courage, open-mindedness, kind-heartedness and a willingness to learn – all of which he has in abundance! George does have something that no one else does ... simply, that George is George and we all took to him like a duck to water. Keep on quacking! Much love!

Mikyla Jane Durkan
Artistic Director, Burjesta Theatre/Potentially Brilliant Productions

George is ... an open book, heart-on-sleeve, no frills, full of thrills unique character. I'm slowly collecting a ream of 'George-isms' to accompany his next book in case anyone needs a glossary of terms or definitions of his quirky, creative words and phrases he invents. He says he is a 'shylent' protester – someone who is subtle in getting their thoughts out into the world through his verse and penned observations – but he drives home his message and tickles you with his humour with such youthful eagerness and earnest you cannot fail to be affected.
He is the 'Dad I never had' and we adopted each other through the love of performance poetry and he has been there as a good friend, fellow wordsmith and comedy partner in crime ever since.

Sharon Lowe
Poet, Performer & Playwright

I met George a good few years ago and I asked him if he had any recordings of his poems, after hearing him recite some of his work. He said no, so I suggested I could produce and record a CD of his poetry with some backing music and effects. He agreed and decided to give all monies from any sales to charity, which, if you know George or have ever met him, is the obvious thing he would do. He is one of the most compassionate and caring people I have ever met and I am honoured to know him.

George is a very humble man, but this is my bit, so I can tell you he has spent a large part of his life helping the sick and disabled around the Wigan area. He has a heart of gold and is one of those people who really does care about others. He observes life from his own experiences and has an amazing way of turning those experiences into poetic rhyme with a Wigan twist; sometimes full of humour and at other times he has the ability to bring you to tears ('Mi Grandad' and 'Holiday', being two good examples). I hope George doesn't mind me telling you this story, but when he recorded 'Holiday', it was only the second time he had ever read that poem since he wrote it. It tells the story of the tragic death of his son Stephen. The emotion in the recording is immense and the tears were rolling down his face and it never fails to hit home every time I listen to it. George has become a lifelong friend and also a surrogate 'Mi Grandad' to me and he genuinely is one of the nicest people I have ever met. He won't like me saying this but, it's all true! Great to see you releasing your first book George and now you have your CD under your belt it's just the film to come!

Stephen Houghton
Musician, Producer & friend

With thanks to

John Togher and the gang at
Wigan Write Out Loud
for giving this 'Owd Chap a voice,

and
all mi poetry families spread far and wide,

and everyone who's encouraged me
with mi writing.